WONDERFUL
WORLD OF
ANIMALS

For a free color catalog describing Gareth Stevens' list of high-quality books and multimedia programs, call 1-800-542-2595 (USA) or 1-800-461-9120 (Canada). Gareth Stevens Publishing's Fax: (414) 225-0377.
See our catalog, too, on the World Wide Web: http://gsinc.com

Library of Congress Cataloging-in-Publication Data

MacLeod, Beatrice.
    Mammals / text by Beatrice MacLeod ; illustrated by Ivan Stalio.
      p. cm. -- (Wonderful world of animals)
    Includes bibliographical references (p. 31) and index.
    Summary: Introduces the physical characteristics, behavior, and habitat
of various mammals.
    ISBN 0-8368-1957-8 (lib. bdg.)
    1. Mammals--Juvenile literature. [1. Mammals.] I. Stalio, Ivan, ill.
II. Title. III. Series: MacLeod, Beatrice. Wonderful world of animals.
QL706.2.M235 1997
599--dc21   97-20190

This North American edition first published in 1997 by
Gareth Stevens Publishing
1555 North RiverCenter Drive, Suite 201
Milwaukee, Wisconsin 53212 USA

This U.S. edition © 1997 by Gareth Stevens, Inc. Created and produced with original © 1996 by McRae Books, Srl, Via dei Rustici, 5 - Florence, Italy. Additional end matter © 1997 by Gareth Stevens, Inc.

Text: Beatrice MacLeod
Design: Marco Nardi
Illustrations: Ivan Stalio
U.S. Editor: Patricia Lantier-Sampon
Editorial assistants: Diane Laska, Rita Reitci

Note: Beatrice MacLeod has a Bachelor of Science degree in Biology. She works as a freelance journalist for Italian nature magazines and also writes children's nonfiction books on nature.

Printed in the United States of America

1 2 3 4 5 6 7 8 9 01 00 99 98 97

WONDERFUL WORLD OF ANIMALS

MAMMALS

Text by Beatrice MacLeod
Illustrations by Ivan Stalio

Gareth Stevens Publishing
MILWAUKEE

WHAT IS A MAMMAL?

Gorillas and cats are mammals. So are people, kangaroos, bats, mice, dolphins, and lots of other animals. What do they all have in common? All mammals are warm-blooded. They nearly all give birth to live young, instead of laying eggs. They feed their babies milk. They nearly all have body hair.

Cats are often kept as pets. Sometimes farmers keep them to hunt mice in their barns. Cats are special because they are the only mammals that purr when they are happy or contented.

Domestic cat

Mountain gorillas live in the mountainous rain forests of central Africa. They are a highly endangered species.

Mountain gorilla

The most intelligent mammals
Humans are the most intelligent mammals. The next most intelligent are the apes. There are five ape species: gorillas, chimpanzees, orangutans, gibbons, and siamangs. Some apes have been taught to speak using sign language.

Mammals Live...

Mammals live in the country, in cities and towns, in forests and deserts, and in rivers, lakes, and oceans. They have evolved in so many different ways that at least some species can survive in every environment in the world.

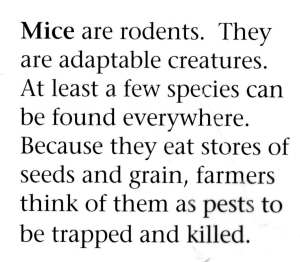

Harvest mice

Mice are rodents. They are adaptable creatures. At least a few species can be found everywhere. Because they eat stores of seeds and grain, farmers think of them as pests to be trapped and killed.

Almost all **monkeys** live in tropical forests. They spend their lives in the treetops. They have long tails and arms for gripping branches and swinging. The howler monkey is a very noisy animal.

Howler monkey

Bottle-nosed dolphin

Dolphins live in seas and oceans, and sometimes in rivers, too. They stay together in groups. They are intelligent, playful, and friendly animals.

THEY ALSO LIVE . . .

Some mammals can survive almost anywhere. Others have special features to help them live in difficult or extreme environments.

Dromedary, or one-humped camel

Camels live in the desert. They can survive for several weeks without food and about one week without water. They store fat in their humps, which they use when there is no food.

The **ibex** is a member of the goat family. It lives high up among the mountain peaks. It is an agile climber. Ibexes eat plants that grow on steep slopes. These slopes are too difficult for other animals to reach.

Ibex

Ships of the desert

Before modern highways and airplanes were invented, camels were used to transport goods and people across deserts. Many camels traveling together were called "caravans." In some parts of the world, such as North Africa and Arabia, camels are still used for transportation.

Mammals Eat . . .

Some mammals feed on the flesh of other animals. They are called carnivores. Other mammals eat plants, and they are called herbivores. Yet others eat both plants and animals, and they are called omnivores.

Lions are carnivores. Lionesses do most of the hunting. They usually attack young, old, or sick animals that are easier to catch than healthy, full-grown ones. They drag the prey back to the pride.

Lion

Brown bears are omnivores. They eat plants, roots, berries, insects, fish, small mammals, and carrion.

Brown bear or Grizzly

Giraffe

The tallest mammal in the world is an herbivore. **Giraffes** grow to about 18 feet (5.5 meters) tall. Their very long legs and neck allow them to feed on the succulent topmost branches and leaves that other animals can't reach.

PICKY EATERS

Some mammals have special diets. They may feed on just one kind of food. Being a picky, or "specialist," eater is not a problem as long as there is plenty of the preferred food in the area.

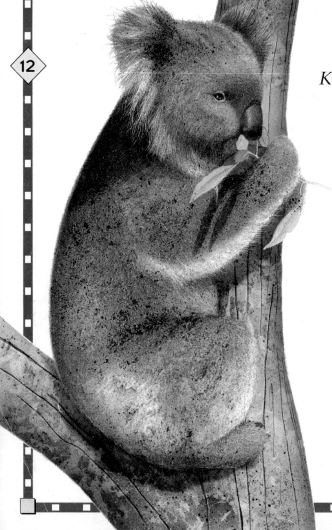

Koala

Koalas live in Australia. They eat eucalyptus leaves. These leaves are poisonous for most other herbivores, but koalas can neutralize the poison. They spend their whole lives in the trees on which they feed.

Giant pandas are very rare animals. They live in dense bamboo forests in China. They feed almost exclusively on bamboo shoots and roots.

Giant panda

Endangered animals

When a species of animal becomes rare, we say it is endangered. This means it is at risk of becoming extinct. Many animals are endangered because people destroy their environments to clear land for farming or forestry. Specialist feeders are often threatened in this way. Hunting is another major threat.

MAMMALS IN THE WATER

Some mammals live all their lives in oceans, lakes, or rivers. They include seals, whales, dolphins, and walruses. Others, such as the hippopotamus, spend a great deal of time in the water but come ashore to feed.

Hippopotamus

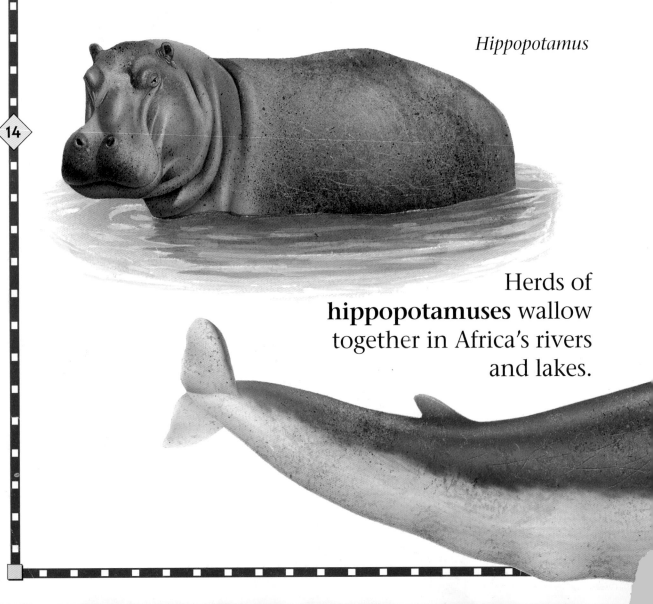

Herds of **hippopotamuses** wallow together in Africa's rivers and lakes.

Sea lions spend most of their lives at sea. They have thick fur coats with a layer of fat, or blubber, underneath. The blubber keeps them warm in the water. Sea lions belong to one of the seal families.

Sea lion

The **blue whale** is the largest mammal. Whales are part of the same group as dolphins. They live at sea. They have special streamlined bodies that help them move quickly through the water.

Blue whale

DOMESTIC MAMMALS

Many mammals live on farms or in houses with people. They are known as domestic mammals because their ancestors were "domesticated," or tamed, by people thousands of years ago. Dogs were probably the first animals to be domesticated.

Foal

Before cars, trucks, trains, and airplanes were invented, **horses** were the main means of travel and transportation. Today they are kept mainly for sport and pleasure.

Sheep and goats were among the first animals people tamed. They are kept by farmers all over the world. They produce wool for clothing, milk for drinking and for making cheese, and meat for eating.

Italian sheep

Domestic pig

Domestic pigs are much larger than their wild relatives. This is because humans have used selective breeding, which means choosing the largest and strongest to mate with others of the same kind. Pigs can make a lot of noise, including squeaks, grunts, and chirrups.

Baby Mammals

Newborn mammals need special care. Sometimes, mammal parents care for their young for many years, teaching them how to survive and protecting them from danger. Elephants and humans look after their offspring for the longest time.

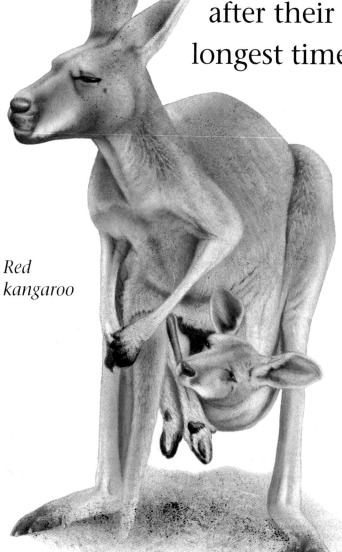

Red kangaroo

Kangaroos are marsupials. Female kangaroos give birth to tiny babies that develop in a pouch on their belly. Baby kangaroos, called joeys, stay in the pouch or return to it to nurse until they are about two years old.

African elephant

A mother **African elephant** has to wait nearly two years for her baby to be born. Then she spends several years teaching it to take care of itself.

Cat and kittens

Female cats can have up to ten kittens at a time. Mother cats groom and feed the babies every day until they are old enough to care for themselves.

HAVING FUN

Mammal babies spend a part of each day leaping, chasing each other, and play-fighting. Playing strengthens their muscles, teaches them to coordinate eyes and paws, and develops other useful skills for hunting and defense.

Red foxes

Growing **foxes** battle it out with brothers and sisters, learning lessons about defending themselves in a safe situation.

Even full-grown animals often spend time playing. Pet **dogs** and cats have a lot of extra energy to burn up because they don't have to hunt for their meals.

Terrier

Growing up and learning

Some mammals grow up very quickly and can take care of themselves soon after birth. Young antelope and other grassland herbivores can keep up with the herd just an hour after they are born. They must be able to do this; otherwise, they will be eaten by predators. Many young mammals get lessons from their parents.

BLENDING IN

Being hard to see can be useful, both to escape predators or to creep up on unwary prey. For this reason, many mammals are the same color as their surrounding environment. Some even change color with the seasons, so they are always hard to spot.

Creamy white or yellow **polar bears** blend in perfectly with the snowy arctic landscape in which they live.

Polar bear cubs

The **arctic hare** is white in winter, so hungry foxes and owls have a hard time seeing it in the snow. In spring, the hare's coat turns brown. This makes it harder to see against the summer grass and lichens.

Arctic hare

Tigers live in Asia. Their stripes are useful for moving unseen in shady, dappled forests and grasslands.

Tiger

RESTING

All mammals spend a part of each day resting or sleeping. Some, such as sloths and bats, sleep for about twenty hours. Others, such as elephants and antelopes, need only a few hours rest.

Zebras live on Africa's open grasslands. They are vulnerable to predators and need to stay alert all the time. They take short naps throughout the day and are always ready to jump up and run away.

Zebra

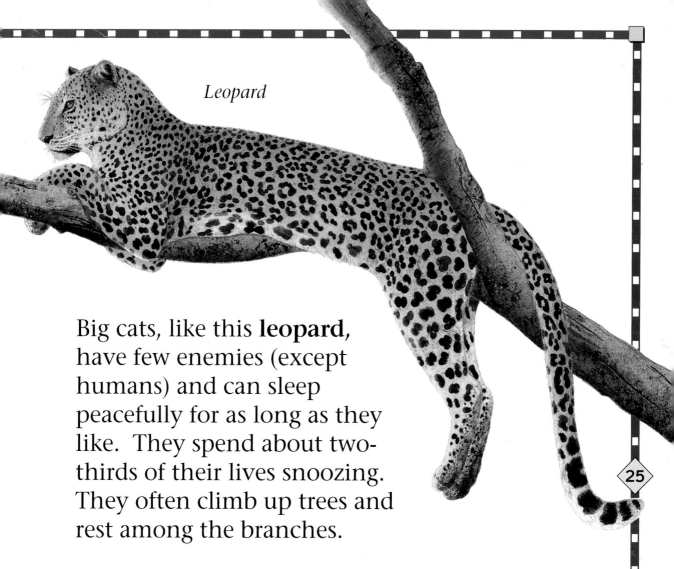

Leopard

Big cats, like this **leopard**, have few enemies (except humans) and can sleep peacefully for as long as they like. They spend about two-thirds of their lives snoozing. They often climb up trees and rest among the branches.

Hibernation

Some mammals take longer periods of rest, usually in winter when food is scarce. During summer and fall they eat well, building up stores of fat. As winter begins, they snuggle into a nest or den and fall asleep. During hibernation, their heartbeat and breathing slow down and body temperature drops.

SPECIAL MAMMALS

Some mammals are survivors from another age and are more closely related to extinct animals than anything alive today. Others have skills that are unique in the animal kingdom. This makes them special and sometimes difficult to recognize as mammals.

The **aardvark** has a piglike body; a long snout; huge, floppy ears; and a strong, muscular tail. It is a living fossil. Its closest relative is the elephant!

Aardvark

Bats are the only mammals that can fly. Many bats also have a kind of built-in radar system, called echolocation, which they use to hunt in the dark.

Platypuses are one of just two groups of mammals that lay soft-shelled, reptile-like eggs.

*Australian
platypus*

GLOSSARY

adaptable: able to adjust behavior or needs to survive in changing conditions.

agile: able to move quickly and easily.

blubber: thick fat that keeps an animal warm by trapping heat inside its body.

caravan: a train or line of pack animals that travel together, usually across a desert or other terrain.

carnivores: meat-eating animals.

carrion: dead and decaying flesh.

den: the lair or shelter of a wild animal.

echolocation: also called a bat's "radar," this is how a bat navigates. Bats send out sounds that bounce, or echo, off their sur-roundings. This gives them a sound-picture of their location, distance from objects, and the size of their prey.

endangered: at risk of dying out completely.

environment: the surroundings in which plants, animals, and other organisms live.

evolve: to change shape or develop gradually over time.

extinct: no longer alive.

fossils: remains or traces of an animal or plant from long ago often found in rock or in Earth's crust.

groom *(v)*: to clean or to tend.

herbivores: plant-eating animals.

herd: a group of animals that travel together.

hibernation: a state of rest or inactivity during the winter, in which the body functions of some animals slow down.

lichens: plants that are formed from a combination of fungi (such as mushrooms, molds, and mildew) and algae (plants that grow in water and do not have roots, leaves, or stems).

mammals: warm-blooded animals that nurse their young with milk from their own bodies. Mammals always have some hair or fur on their bodies.

marsupials: animals whose young are born not fully developed. The babies complete their development in a pouch on the mother's belly. Kangaroos are marsupials.

offspring: the babies, or young, of plants and animals.

omnivores: animals that eat both plants and other animals.

predators: animals that hunt and kill other animals for food.

prey: animals that are hunted and killed for food by other animals.

pride: a group of lions that live and hunt together.

rain forest: a tropical wooded area that has at least 100 inches (254 centimeters) of rain a year.

snout: protruding nose and jaw of an animal.

species: animals or plants that are closely related and often similar in behavior or appearance.

vulnerable: in a position or situation that is open to danger or attack by predators.

wallow: to roll around, especially in mud.

ACTIVITIES

1. On a trip to a large aquarium or a museum, find out which animals living in water are mammals. How can you tell the difference between these mammals and the fish? How do the mammals breathe? What do they eat? Are the young born in water or on land?

2. Make a miniature museum display. Choose an animal for your exhibit. Ask a grown-up to help you cut away two sides of a sturdy box that touch each other. Now use poster paints, crayons, or colored construction paper to make a scene in which your animal lives, such as a desert, a rain forest, or a woodland. You can paint a sky inside your box, a grassland or desert on the bottom, or a forest along the sides. Cut trees out of construction paper and paste them along the sides, or use twigs stuck in clay with paper leaves. Paint a pond or a stream if your animal needs it. Make your animal out of clay, papier-mâché, or construction paper and place it in its habitat. You might want to add other animals, such as predators or prey.

3. You are traveling in an unexplored country when a tremendous rainstorm forces you to run into a cave for shelter. You might have to spend the night there, so you need to know if any mammals share your cave. Using your flashlight, you go deep into the cave, searching tunnels, cracks, ledges, and even ceilings. What kinds of mammals would you expect to find living in the cave? What would they eat, and how would they find food? Think of a way to spend the night safely in the cave.

Books and Videos

Animal Families series. (Gareth Stevens)

Animals of the Night. (Wood Knapp Video)

Endangered Mammals! ENDANGERED! series. Bob Burton (Gareth Stevens)

Forest Animals. (Kimbo Educational video)

Giant Animals. (Wood Knapp Video)

Insect Eaters. (International Film Bureau)

Mammoth. Heather Amery (Gareth Stevens)

Paws, Wings, and Hooves: Mammals on the Move. Keiko Yamashita (Lerner Group)

A Picture Book of Underwater Life. Theresa Grace (Troll Communications)

Polar Mammals. (Children's Press)

Secrets of the Animal World series. (Gareth Stevens)

Twenty-five Mammals Every Child Should Know. Jim Arnosky (Simon & Schuster Children's)

What Is a Mammal? Robert Snedden (Sierra)

The World of Mammals. (Kimbo Educational video)

Web Sites

www.olcommerce.com/terra/land.html

www.bhm.tis.net/zoo/views/

www.yahoo.com/Science/Zoology/Animals_Insects_and_Pets/Mammals/

INDEX